GW00363587

LEISURE LIBRARY
✳
COCKTAILS

CONTENTS

—— ❊ ——

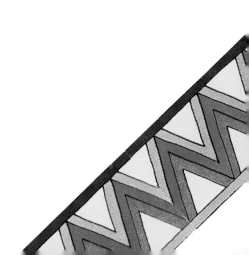

INTRODUCTION

*W*hat makes a good party? The right mix of people, good food and of course the drinks. A good host always has the right drink for every guest, taking care to cater to the taste and style of the person.

Early in the 20th century people began to find regular drinks too commonplace. And there were times when the customary champagne, wine or beer just did not suit the occasion. By experimenting with drinks, it became possible to create heady concoctions by mixing different liquors which were in stock. The new concoctions, which came to be known as cocktails, were so popular that they became a symbol of sophisticated society, and an essential part of high living, Great Gatsby style. Cocktails are basically alcohol-based drinks which are combined with soft drinks, fruit juices, liqueurs and tonics or flavoured with bitters, to give an exotic high.

Why the name cocktail is a question that is still debated all over the world, perhaps as often as the drink is imbibed. There are as many stories to the origins of the word as there are cocktails. A Bordeaux wine cup is called a Coquetel. Is that where the word cocktail comes from? Some say it comes from *coquetiers,* or egg cups in which a French eccentric used to serve drinks to his friends. Others say it is from the rooster's tail feathers that were used to stir mixed drinks in Mississippi; a barmaid is once said to have mixed drinks and stored them in bottles decorated with cock's feathers; or possibly it has been named after the 18th century mixture of drinks—Cockale—served to fighting cocks just before a fight. And then there is the wild story of how mixed breed horses have cocked tails and hence the name for mixed drinks.

Whatever the origins of the word, the concept came in very handy during the Prohibition era in the United States. The liquor available was so unpalatable that it could only be consumed by disguising it. After the Prohibition era, the cocktail made its way across the Atlantic to Europe.

Today cocktails are imbibed all over the world. There are thousands of cocktails and each one has innumerable variations depending on individual tastes, local flavours and ingredients. Making and serving a cocktail has become an art. Every barman prides himself on his own special blends.

There are a few basic guidelines to making a cocktail. The ingredients should be blended together to get the right texture and look. Opaque or cloudy ingredients should be shaken in a cocktail shaker. Drinks with clear ingredients should be stirred . When separate and distinct colours are required, the ingredients should be added gently with a spoon. Garnish and decorate the cocktail to enhance its flavour and give it visual appeal.

Use this book as a basic guide. You can innovate and experiment to create your own concoctions. There is no right or wrong way to make a cocktail. A home bartender has the freedom to experiment and offer his guests exotic drinks that stimulate the senses.

EQUIPMENT

*7*he equipment in your cocktail bar depends on how worthwhile an investment you consider it to be. Most of the items can be improvised from the kitchen though it would boost your cocktail making skills immensely if you had some of the basic tools of the trade. A barman is taken as seriously as he takes himself. Cocktail straws, sticks and parasols are used for the garnishes. Stirrers and coasters are useful when serving the drinks.

Bottle opener: Use a multipurpose device which opens corks, crowns and cans. The best corkscrews have spiral screws coated with a non-stick substance to make them slip easily through the cork.

Bar spoon: A bar spoon is the size of a teaspoon with a long slim handle. The other end has a flat metal disc. The spoon is used to stir the ingredients settled at the bottom of the glass. The disc is used for crushing ice, sugar or any other solid ingredients.

Ice crusher: Used mainly for crushing ice but a specialised one can also be used for cracking or shaving ice.

Ice container: You need a spacious and well-insulated ice bucket. For white wines and champagne a bucket ice container is needed.

Measure: Different measures are used in different parts of the world. The Americans use the fluid ounces and the Europeans the gills and the centilitres.

Mixing glasses: Mixing glasses are used for clear drinks. Once stirred the drink should be strained before pouring into a cocktail glass. Usually a mixing glass is equipped with a strainer and a coil spring around it so that the ice does not fall into the glass.

Shaker: This is the most important equipment and can be either of silver or steel. It has a strainer in the top chamber which simplifies the serving of the drinks. The shaker is used mainly for drinks made with fruit juices, syrups, or a very thick liqueur base.

Paring knife, chopping board: A sharp knife is a handy tool to create cocktails. It is used for cutting slivers and twists of lemon or cucumber peel, slices of oranges and to trim other garnishes.

Jugs: A jug with an involuted pourer to hold back the ice cubes is required for water or fruit juice.

Lemon squeezer: Juices add tangy flavouring to the drinks. For a large party store and keep plenty of juice.

Tongs: It is more elegant to use tongs than a spoon to fish ice out of a bucket, and to avoid excess water being added.

Strainers: Use strainers that clip on to the edge of the mixing glass.

GLASSES

CHAMPAGNE TULIP

CHAMPAGNE SAUCER

MARTINI GLASS

PARIS GOBLET

*C*ocktail glasses come in a variety of shapes and sizes, not only to bring out to best effect the visual appeal of the drink but also its flavour. As any connoisseur will tell you this helps to retain the aromas, to heighten the bouquet and above all to allow one to enjoy the drink better. Stemmed glasses are used for chilled drinks so that they do not become warm as you hold them. Tall glasses are used for the fruit punches and/or layered drinks, showing off their colours to best advantage.

Champagne: There are two kinds of champagne glasses—the tall narrow tulip-shaped Champagne Flute, and the Champagne Saucer. The wide surface area of the saucer allows space for the garnish in the champagne-based cocktails, while the Champagne Flute is far more aesthetic and suitable for this sparkling wine.

Martini: A classic V-shaped glass that one associates with sophistication. Ideal to serve Martinis and Margaritas.

Paris Goblet: A standard, solid red wine glass that suits Burgandy wine. The well-rounded balloon shaped bowl and the short stem can be held and kept warm by the hand. The rim is just wide enough to let the wine breathe.

White Wine: A glass with a long stem ideal for chilled drinks. The narrow bowl keeps the drink cooler for a longer period. These glasses if refrigerated prior to filling get a

10

WHITE WINE GLASS

frostiness which gives the drink a stylish charm.

Brandy Balloon/Sniffer: Used for brandy or brandy-based cocktails. The well-rounded shape allows you to hold the glass snugly to keep the drink warm. The wide balloon of the shape makes the aroma of the contents rise to top of the glass, and holds the powerful bouquet to be sniffed and enjoyed leisurely.

BRANDY BALLOON

Highball/Collins: Ideal for long, fruity drinks—the taller the better. The cylindrical straight sides of the tumbler-like glass show off to delectable perfection the vibrant colours of fruit punches or layered drinks.

HIGHBALL

Lowball: A multipurpose short tumbler, used to serve a variety of drinks. Ideally its tapering shape is suited to serving a Bloody Mary.

Old-fashioned: Can be used for any of the traditional cocktails served on the rocks and also as a whiskey glass.

LOWBALL

Cocktail: This is the most widely used glass on the cocktail circuit. It is an elegant, well proportioned glass with a long stem that prevents the drink from becoming too warm. The bowl has flaring sides wide enough to display the garnish.

There are numerous other glasses which are used for special types of cocktails. Among these are the commonly used Balloon glass, whose well rounded shape holds the aroma and its depth makes it ideal for garnishes and ice. The Volcano Bowl is generally used for flambé cocktails.

OLD-FASHIONED

COCKTAIL

11

PRESENTATION

※

*E*very host who enjoys his drink would like his guests to have a special drink to remember. The scope for creativity in making your own cocktail is tremendous.

The classic cocktail was a short dryish drink using whiskey, gin or brandy. But as cocktails became popular in other parts of the world other liqueurs were tried out, like rum and the wines. The latest additions are tequila, and vodka which add a fiery kick to a fruit based drink. An ideal cocktail is where the base drink can clearly be distinguished.

Apart from the spirits, the liqueurs used in cocktails are: Cointreau, creme de menthe, curaçao, Bénédictine, advocaat and kirsch. The wines used are: sherry, port, vermouth, champagne, sparkling wine, red, rose and white wine.

Tonics, sodas, bitter lemon, ginger ale, tomato juice and fresh fruit juices serve as mixers. Worcestershire sauce, tabasco, Angostura bitters, grenadine, lime juice, mint cordial and gomme syrup (sugar syrup), cream, honey and cold tea give flavour. Ice serves to chill, dilute and act as a beater. Crushed ice cools a drink, and is used for drinks to be sipped with a straw. Ice cubes are used for drinks on the rocks. Shaved ice is used to create any icy slush.

Tall glasses are sometimes

frosted to give an exotic touch or an additional flavouring. To frost the rim of the glass dip into a saucer of egg white and then sugar, or into lemon juice and salt. To get a pink frosting dip into pomegranate syrup and then sugar.

Other popular garnishes include oranges, cherries for their colour, olives for their savoury tang, mint leaves, slices of kiwi fruit, strawberries, pineapple, cucumbers, slices of apricots, strawberries and mangoes. All garnishes must be fresh.

Swizzle sticks, plastic straws, paper parasols, and the like, can be used for stirring or holding garnishes. Whether a drink should be stirred, shaken or poured depends on the ingredients. Drinks with clear ingredients should be stirred. Add the ingredients to ice cubes in the mixing glass, stir with a bar spoon and strain. Drinks with cloudier ingredients—fruit juices, egg whites, or cream—should be shaken or blended. Put all ingredients with ice into a shaker and shake rapidly with quick, short, vertical movements. Strain and discard ice. If using a blender make sure you blend only for a few seconds or the drink may become too diluted. To get a layered drink, pour each liqueur into a dessertspoon and gently tip so that the liquid slips on to the surface of the drink.

The visual appeal of a cocktail is of paramount importance and if you have the right ingredients, the possibilities of inventing your own drink are immense.

Grasshopper

GRASSHOPPER

A popular delightful cocktail.

Ingredients

30 ml brandy
15 ml Cacao White
15 ml green crème de menthe
5 ml fresh lime
10 ml fresh cream
Glass: Champagne Saucer
Garnish: Mint sprig

Steps

1. Pour all the ingredients into a Boston shaker,
add two to three cubes of ice and shake well.
2. Strain into a glass and add mint sprig.

B&B

Named so from the first alphabet of the basic spirits used.

Ingredients

30 ml brandy
30 ml Bénédictine
Glass: Brandy Sniffer
Garnish: None

Steps

1. Pour the two liqueurs into the glass and stir.
2. Serve without ice.

Gin Fizz

GIN FIZZ

As the name suggests the drink should fizz, so blend the mixture well with crushed ice and employ the soda siphon with some gusto. A bottle of soda won't do.

Ingredients

60 ml gin
10 ml fresh lime juice
10 ml sugar syrup
Dash egg white
Soda to top up
Glass: Highball
Garnish: Half a slice each of orange and lime and a cherry

Steps

1. Blend all the ingredients except the soda with two to three cubes of ice.
2. Pour the mixture into the glass and top it with soda.
3. Serve garnished with the orange and lime slice and the cherry.

WHITE LADY

There are several versions of this elegant little drink. Some use vodka as a base, but gin is the most popular starting point.

Ingredient

30 ml gin
15 ml Cointreau
15 ml lemon juice
½ an egg white
Ice cubes
Glass: Cocktail
Garnish: None

Steps

1. Place the gin, Cointreau, lemon juice and egg white in a cocktail shaker with four ice cubes.
2. Shake very well, then strain into a cocktail glass. Serve undecorated.

17

Thundering Typhoon

THUNDERING TYPHOON

Bartender's own creation.

Ingredients

60 ml gin
30 ml orange juice
10 ml fresh lime juice
10 ml sugar syrup
Dash of egg white
Crushed ice
Glass: Champagne Saucer
Garnish: Peeled orange slice

Steps

1. Blend all ingredients well and serve on crushed ice.
2. Garnish with orange slice.

GIMLET

One of the classics that has numerous variations.

Ingredients

60 ml gin
30 ml lime juice cordial
Crushed ice
Glass: Cocktail
Garnish: A slice of lime

Steps

1. Place three tablespoons of crushed ice in a cocktail shaker.
2. Add the gin and lime juice and shake well.
3. Strain into a cocktail glass.
4. Decorate with a slice of lime and serve with a pretty straw.

Million Dollar

MILLION DOLLAR

Gives a heady feeling of having a million dollars.

Ingredients

30 ml gin
30 ml sweet vermouth
10 ml fresh lime juice
5 ml grenadine syrup
Dash of egg white
30 ml pineapple juice
Glass: Champagne Tulip
Garnish: Pineapple and cherry

Steps

1. Put two to three cubes of ice into a cocktail shaker and add all the ingredients.
2. Shake well, stir, and pour into the glass with the garnish on top. Serve.

FLYING DUTCHMAN

A variation of the Dry Martini

Ingredients

45 ml ice cold Jenever gin
1 tsp Dutch curaçao
Dash of orange bitters
Glass: Cocktail, chilled
Garnish: None

Steps

1. Put the curaçao into a chilled glass and swirl around.
2. Empty the glass. Pour in the gin and add the bitters. Serve.

Tom Colli

TOM COLLINS

Named after the New York locality where it was first drunk in the 1890s, this drink was originally made with Old Tom gin, the best known amongst the brand of sweetened gins.

Ingredients

60 ml gin
10 ml fresh lime juice
10 ml sugar syrup
Soda to top up
Glass: Collins
Garnish: Lime slice and cherry

Steps

1. Pour all the ingredients into a Collins glass, stir well and top up with soda.
2. Stir again and add the garnish and serve.

BRONX

A relic of the American Prohibition era.

Ingredients

60 ml dry gin
30 ml orange juice
15 ml dry vermouth
15 ml sweet vermouth
Ice cubes
Glass: Cocktail
Garnish: None

Steps

1. Pour all the ingredients into a shaker along with four ice cubes and shake well.
2. Strain into a Cocktail glass and serve.

23

Dry Martini

Dry Martini

Said to be invented for John D. Rockefeller by a bartender, Martini, of New York.

Ingredients

60 ml gin
Dash (2 to 3 drops) dry vermouth
Glass: Cocktail, frosted
Garnish: Stuffed olive/green olive

Steps

1. Pour the gin into a cocktail shaker.
2. Add dash of vermouth and two to four cubes of ice. Stir well so that no flavour dominates.
3. Garnish with olive.

Blue Hawai

Named after a famous dancer.

Ingredients

30 ml gin
15 ml blue curaçao
5 ml coconut cream
60 ml pineapple juice
10 ml fresh lime
10 ml sugar syrup
Soda
Glass: Collins
Garnish: None

Steps

1. Mix gin, blue curaçao, coconut cream and pineapple juice in a shaker. Shake well, adding fresh lime and sugar syrup.
2. Pour into a Collins glass.
3. Add crushed ice. Top with soda.

Pink Lady

PINK LADY

A variation of the more traditional White Lady.

Ingredients

45 ml gin
15 ml Cointreau
10 ml fresh lime juice
5 ml grenadine syrup
5-10 ml fresh cream
Castor sugar to frost the rim of the glass
Glass: Champagne Saucer
Garnish: A cherry

Steps

1. Pour some syrup in a saucer and add castor sugar.
2. Roll the rim of the frosted Champagne Saucer in the syrup.
3. Pour all the ingredients into the blender and blend well. Strain into glass and serve.

SKYSCRAPER

Reminds one of a high rise building.

Ingredients

45 ml gin
Dash green crème de menthe
15 ml Cointreau
15 ml fresh lime juice
10 ml sugar syrup
Egg white
Mint leaves, crushed
Crushed ice
Soda as required
Glass: Collins
Garnish: Mint leaves and slice of lime

Steps

1. Pour all the ingredients in the blender except the soda. Blend well and pour the mixture into the glass.
2. Add crushed ice and fill with soda.
3. Garnish with mint leaves and lime slice.

SINGAPORE SLING

A sweetish long drink, containing cherry brandy.

Ingredients

45 ml gin
15 ml cherry brandy
10 ml fresh lime juice
5 ml sugar syrup
Crushed ice
Soda as required
Glass: Highball
Garnish: Half a slice each of orange and lime and one cherry

Steps

1. Pour all the ingredients into the glass, add crushed ice and top it up with soda.
2. Stir and serve, garnishing with the orange, lemon and cherry.

General's Salute

General's Salute

A refreshing cocktail, which is the barman's creation.

Ingredients

45 ml tequila
15 ml Crème de Cassis
10 ml fresh lime juice
10 ml sugar syrup
Dash of egg white
Crushed ice
Glass: Champagne Tulip (crystal)
Garnish: Lime slice and cherry

Steps

1. Salt the rim of the glass (see p. 13).
2. Shake all the ingredients well in the shaker and strain into the glass, adding crushed ice.
3. Garnish with slice of lime and cherry and serve.

Galliano Sour

An unusual blend of whiskey and orange juice.

Ingredients

30 ml Scotch whiskey
30 ml Galliano
30 ml orange juice
Castor sugar
½ lemon or lime juice
Ice cubes
Glass: Cocktail
Garnish: A slice of orange

Steps

1. Place eight ice cubes in a cocktail shaker and add all the liquid ingredients.
2. Shake well.
3. Frost the rim of a cocktail glass with castor sugar (see p. 13), strain the cocktail carefully into the glass, taking care not to disturb the frosting.
4. Decorate with the orange slice.

Blue Margarita

BLUE MARGARITA

Said to be named after a Mexican dancer.

Ingredients

15 ml blue curaçao
45 ml white tequila
10 ml fresh lime juice
10 ml sugar syrup
Dash of egg white
Glass: Champagne Saucer
Garnish: A slice of lime and a cherry

Steps

1. Pour all the ingredients into the blender and blend well.
2. Salt the rim of the glass (see p. 13) and pour in the mixture.
3. Garnish with the slice of lime and the cherry on a cocktail stick.

AARON

Hebrew word for high mountains. Romantically it also means 'with love'.

Ingredients

30 ml vodka
15 ml Creme de Cassis
15 ml Baileys Irish Cream
10 ml fresh cream
Dash of grenadine syrup
Glass: Champagne Tulip
Garnish: Cherry

Steps

1. Mix all the ingredients. Shake well so as to merge all flavours.
2. Pour into the glass. Top with crushed ice. Garnish with cherry.

Kir Royale

KIR ROYALE

An exotic champagne cocktail.

Ingredients

125 ml Champagne
10 ml Creme de Cassis
Glass: Champagne Tulip
Garnish: None

Steps

1. Pour champagne into a Tulip glass.
2. Top with Creme de Cassis.

LACRIME DAL CIELO

Tear's from Heaven. Named so by the barman after the song by Eric Clapton.

Ingredients

15 ml cognac
15 ml Cointreau
15 ml Campari
30 ml grape juice
5 ml sugar syrup
10 ml fresh lime juice
Crushed ice
Rose Champagne as required
Glass: Champagne Saucer
Garnish: Half a pineapple slice and one cherry

Steps

1. Blend all the ingredients well except the champagne.
2. Pour into the Champagne Saucer and add Rose Champagne to fill the glass.
3. Garnish with slice of pineapple and cherry and serve.

Vesuvio Fieroso

Vesuvio Fieroso

A drink as fiery as Mt. Vesuvius.

Ingredients

45 ml Calvados
15 ml orange curaçao
30 ml grapefruit juice
10 ml fresh lime juice
5 ml sugar syrup
Glass: Cocktail
Garnish: Pineapple slice with a cherry inserted in it.

Steps

1. Pour all the ingredients in a cocktail shaker and add two to three cubes of ice. Shake well. No one ingredient should dominate.
2. Garnish with pineapple slice and cherry and serve.

Americano

Actually an Italian drink, it is served as a sunny apéritif which is also very refreshing.

Ingredients

30 ml Campari
30 ml gin
Glass: Highball, if using soda: Cocktail, if not
Garnish: Lemon or orange peel

Steps

1. Stir the Campari and gin together and pour in the Cocktail glass.
2. Garnish with orange or lemon peel. If soda is added, pour into the Highball glass and garnish as before.

Tequila Sunrise

TEQUILA SUNRISE

The ingredients are poured straight into the glass. The grenadine gives the effect of sunrise.

Ingredients

45 ml tequila
120 ml orange juice
5 ml of grenadine syrup
Glass: Highball
Garnish: One orange slice

Steps

1. Rotate the grenadine syrup into the glass, add ice and orange juice.
2. Pour in the tequila and stir.
3. Garnish with orange slice. Serve.

NEGRONI

An elegant apéritif liqueur.

Ingredients

30 ml Campari
30 ml gin
15 ml sweet vermouth
Glass: Highball, if using soda: Cocktail, if not.
Garnish: Lemon or orange peel

Steps

1. Stir all the ingredients together and pour straight. Add soda if preferred.
2. Garnish with lemon or orange peel.

Egg Nog

Egg Nog

An ideal after dinner drink.

Ingredients

30 ml rum
30 ml brandy
1 egg
Hot milk
15 ml fresh cream
Glass: Wine
Garnish: Pinch of cinnamon

Steps

1. Pour all the ingredients in the shaker and blend vigorously.
2. Add hot milk and stir.
3. Pour in the Wine glass. Sprinkle with cinnamon. Serve.

Mai-Tai

Name is similar to Chinese liquor, but is now a classic cocktail.

Ingredients

15 ml white rum
15 ml dark rum
15 ml brandy
15 ml Cointreau
10 ml fresh lime juice
10 ml sugar syrup
5 ml grenadine syrup
Dash of Angostura bitters
120 ml orange juice
Crushed ice
Glass: Beer Goblet
Garnish: Pineapple wedge and a cherry

Steps

1. Pour all ingredients except orange juice and crushed ice into the Boston Shaker and shake well.
2. Add crushed ice and orange juice.
3. Pour into the Beer Goblet, garnish with the pineapple and cherry and serve.

Planter's Punch

PLANTER'S PUNCH

A classic mixed drink, ideally made with Jamaican dark rum.

Ingredients

60 ml dark rum
60 ml pineapple juice
60 ml orange juice
5 ml fresh lime juice
Glass: Highball
Garnish: Half each of orange and lime slice and cherry

Steps

1. Put two to three cubes of ice into a Highball glass.
2. Add fresh lime, pineapple juice and orange juice.
3. Add the rum so that it floats on top.
4. Garnish and serve.

PINA COLADA

Most popular among mixed drinks.

Ingredients

60 ml white rum
10 ml fresh lime juice
15 ml fresh cream
15 ml coconut milk or cream
120 ml pineapple juice
Glass: Half a small pineapple shell
Garnish: Cherries

Steps

1. Shake all the ingredients so that they are all well blended.
2. Pour the mixture into the pineapple shell.
3. Garnish with cherries.

Black Russian

Black Russian

A stylish after dinner cocktail.

Ingredients

60 ml vodka
15 ml Kahlúa or any coffee liqueur
Ice cubes
Glass: Lowball
Garnish: None

Steps

1. Place a few ice cubes in a cocktail shaker, add the ingredients and shake well.
2. Place several ice cubes in a Lowball glass and strain the contents of the shaker over them.

Harvey Wallbanger

Named after a drunk man who collided with a wall after imbibing this drink.

Ingredients

30 ml vodka
60 ml orange juice
2 tsp Galliano
Ice cubes
Glass: Highball
Garnish: A slice of orange

Steps

1. Place five ice cubes in a cocktail shaker, add the vodka and orange juice and shake well.
2. Strain into a Highball glass and add two cubes of ice.
3. Float two teaspoons of Galliano on the top and decorate with a slice of orange.
4. Serve with a straw.

Screwdriver

SCREWDRIVER

Supposed to be invented by oil men who used screwdrivers to stir the drink.

Ingredients

60 ml vodka
120 ml orange juice
Glass: Highball/or according to the glassware being used
Garnish: Half an orange slice

Steps

1. Mix the orange juice and the vodka in the glass and add two or three cubes of ice. Stir.
2. Decorate rim of glass with half an orange slice.

BLUE LAGOON

Blue drinks always add an exotic touch to a party. This one is no exception.

Ingredients

60 ml vodka
30 ml blue curaçao
60 ml pineapple juice
3 dashes green Chartreuse
Crushed ice
Glass: Lowball
Garnish: A slice of pineapple

Steps

1. Place half a cup of crushed ice in a cocktail shaker and add the vodka, blue curaçao, pineapple juice and green Chartreuse.
2. Shake well and strain into a Lowball glass.
3. Serve decorated with the slice of pineapple.

White Russian

WHITE RUSSIAN

A variation of Black Russian topped with fresh cream.

Ingredients

30 ml vodka
30 ml cafe liqueur
15 ml fresh cream
Glass: Highball
Garnish: Chocolate flakes

Steps

1. Pour the vodka, cafe liqueur and fresh cream into the blender and blend vigorously with two cubes of ice.
2. Strain into the glass.
3. Add chocolate flakes for garnish.

TORRE D'ORO

Named thus because it gives the illusion of being a tower of gold.

Ingredients

45 ml vodka
15 ml Cointreau
½ banana, mashed
10-15 ml fresh cream
120 ml orange juice
5 ml grenadine syrup
Glass: Collins
Garnish: Half a banana and a cherry

Steps

1. Put vodka, cream and mashed banana in a blender and blend.
2. Chill the Collins glass, pour the grenadine in the centre and then roll the glass.
3. Add crushed ice and pour in the banana mixture.
4. Top up with orange juice, add the Cointreau, garnish with banana and cherry. Serve.

BOURBON OLD-FASHIONED

The whiskey must be American, preferably Jack Daniels.

Ingredients

60 ml bourbon
Dash of Angostura bitters
Cube of sugar
60 ml soda
Glass: Old-fashioned or Roly Poly
Garnish: Half an orange slice, a slice of lime and a
cherry

Steps

1. Stir all the ingredients. Pour into Old-fashioned
or Roly Poly glass on the rocks (4 to 5 cubes of
ice).
2. Garnish with the orange and lemon slices
and the cherry and serve.

NEW YORKER

For those who enjoy their drinks slightly sweet.

Ingredients

60 ml bourbon
15 ml lime juice
Dash of grenadine syrup
Glass: Cocktail
Garnish: Twist of orange peel

Steps

1. Shake well the bourbon, lime juice, grenadine
syrup and ice cubes in a shaker.
2. Strain and pour into a Cocktail glass.
3. Garnish with a twist of orange peel and serve.

51

Whiskey Sour

Whiskey Sour

The most classic mixed drink based on spirits, citrus juice and sugar.

Ingredients

60 ml Scotch whiskey
10 ml fresh lime juice
10 ml sugar syrup
Dash egg white
Glass: Collins
Garnish: Lime slice and cherry

Steps

1. Pour all the ingredients into the blender and blend well.
2. Pour into the glass and add the slice of lime and the cherry. Serve.

Rob-Roy

A popular cocktail.

Ingredients

45 ml Scotch whisky
15 ml dry vermouth
Glass: Cocktail
Garnish: Twist of lime

Steps

1. Stir the ingredients with four to five cubes of ice and strain into the glass.
2. Garnish with a twist of lime and serve.

Manhattan

Manhattan

A variation using bourbon instead of rye. One of the basic cocktails, usually made with rye.

Ingredients

45 ml bourbon
15 ml sweet vermouth
Glass: Cocktail
Garnish: A cherry

Steps

1. Stir the ingredients well, adding two to three cubes of ice.
2. Strain into the glass.
3. Add the cherry and serve.

Perfect Manhattan

A Perfect Manhattan is a variation of Dry Manhattan using the same amount of vermouth but half Italian sweet and half French dry.

Ingredients

30 ml rye whiskey
15 ml sweet vermouth
15 ml dry vermouth
Glass: Cocktail
Garnish: Twist of lime

Steps

1. Stir rye whiskey, sweet vermouth and dry vermouth well with ice cubes.
2. Strain into a Cocktail glass.
3. Garnish with a twist of lime.

Rusty-Nail

A drink named after the colour of the Scotch.

Ingredients

30 ml Scotch whiskey
30 ml Drambuie
Dash of Angostura bitters
Glass: Old-fashioned or Roly Poly
Garnish: Twist of lime

Steps

1. Put two to three cubes of ice into the glass and pour in all the ingredients and stir.
2. Serve garnished with a twist of lime.

Mint Julep

An ideal party drink. Can be made in advance.

Ingredients

1 litre bourbon
15 ml rum
2 bunches fresh mint
1 tsp sugar
2 tbs water
Crushed ice
Glass: Beer Goblet
Garnish: Sprigs of mint

Steps

1. Chop mint leaves finely.
2. Pour bourbon into a punch bowl and add the mint leaves.
3. Add the sugar and water and stir until well mixed and the sugar is dissolved.
4. Strain, and pour into another punch bowl. Top with crushed ice and float a teaspoon of rum on the surface.
5. Stir the mixture well. Float remaining rum on the surface.
6. Pour into individual Beer Goblets, garnish and serve

Rusty Nail

Irish Coffee

INDEX

— ✳ —

Emeralda Lily

A refreshing long drink that is perilously alcoholic.

Ingredients

45 ml white rum
15 ml green creme de menthe
10 ml fresh lime
70 ml sugar syrup
120 ml pineapple juice
10 ml fresh cream
Dash of egg white
Crushed mint leaves
Glass: Beer Goblet
Garnish: Half a slice of orange and a sprig of mint

Steps

1. Blend all the ingredients in a blender.
2. Pour into a Beer Goblet.
3. Add crushed ice.
4. Garnish with mint and orange slice and serve.

Mint Fruit Punch

An easy to make, refreshing non-alcoholic drink.

Ingredients

Mint leaves, crushed
Lemon rind, chopped
10 ml fresh lime juice
10 ml sugar syrup
120 ml orange juice
Soda to top up
Glass: Beer Goblet
Garnish: Orange peel, made into an umbrella with a cherry

Steps

1. Pour all the ingredients into a mixer and mix.
2. Pour the mixture into the glass and top it up with soda.
3. Garnish with orange peel. Serve.

ERUPTION

An unusual flambé cocktail.

Ingredients

30 ml brandy
15 ml rum for flambé
10 ml lime juice
15 ml white rum
15 ml blue curaçao
15 ml lime cordial
10 ml sugar syrup
Glass: Volcano Bowl
Garnish: None

Steps

1. Shake all the ingredients together except 15 ml rum for flambé. Pour into the Volcano Bowl.
2. Add crushed ice.
3. In the centre of the bowl pour rum and flambé.

SALTY-DOG

A reviving drink for those who enjoy their drinks sweet.

Ingredients

60 ml vodka
120 ml grapefruit juice
Crushed ice
Glass: Highball with salted rim
Garnish: Grapefruit slice

Steps

1. Pour the juice in the glass, add crushed ice and the vodka and stir.
2. Garnish with grapefruit slice and serve.

Eruption

Irish Coffee

A popular nightcap.

Ingredients

45 ml Irish whiskey
45 ml whipped cream
45 ml hot black coffee
45 ml castor sugar
Glass: Wine
Garnish: Chocolate flakes and a piece of praline

Steps

1. Pour coffee in the glass.
2. Caramelise the sugar by heating in a small saucepan.
3. Add whiskey and stir till sugar melts. Light with a match to flambé.
4. Pour flaming whiskey into the glass.
5. Add whipped cream, a few drops of whiskey and garnish with chocolate flakes and praline.

Cafe Special

A hot drink ideal for a cold winter evening.

Ingredients

30 ml rum
10 ml honey
Pinch of cinnamon
1 tsp coffee powder
1 cup hot water
Glass: A coffee cup
Garnish: 2 tsp whipped cream, 1 tsp chopped walnuts and a dry cherry

Steps

1. Put the honey, cinnamon and coffee powder together in a cup and add a little hot water.
2. Mix well with a spoon and then pour hot water.
3. Add rum and mix again.
4. Garnish with whipped cream, chopped walnuts and top with the cherry.